# INTRODUCTION

MW01036804

# Introduction

## Kratom: The Devil Plant – How to Escape the Green Grip of Hell

In the bustling landscape of wellness and self-improvement, where promises of miraculous solutions often blur the line between hope and hype, there emerged a green powder that's heralded as a panacea.

Kratom—a botanical wonder from the depths of Southeast Asia, with claims that range from soothing anxiety to curbing problematic drinking and drug taking.

Imagine, if you will, stumbling upon what seems like the Holy Grail of wellness—a green powder so mesmerizing it promises to resolve your social anxiety and curb your drinking habits, all while sparing you from the side effects of conventional medicine. If you can imagine this, you'll be picturing me just a few years ago.

My name is Kate Louder and this book serves two purposes; to tell my story of discovering Kratom and falling for its allure, and to provide some helpful tips on how to get away from it, if you're one of those who fell for it too.

Initially, Kratom seemed like the answer to my problems but swiftly became a relentless tormentor.

When I first considered Kratom, I wasn't an alcoholic, but I had begun to notice a creeping issue with my drinking. Social gatherings, once mere annoyances, were becoming battlegrounds where alcohol was my weapon of choice.

My confidence seemed to evaporate in the clamor of social anxiety, and I was starting to rely on drinks to navigate these interactions. Then, in the midst of my quest for a solution, Kratom appeared like a shimmering oasis in a desert of self-help remedies.

The initial encounter was like unwrapping a gift from the universe.

Kratom promised tranquillity and control without the invasive side effects of pharmaceuticals or having to deal with the challenge of going sober.

I envisioned it as my personal magic potion—one that would allow me to enjoy social settings with a newfound sense of calm and perhaps even put an end to my problematic drinking.

The first few weeks felt like living inside a warm, comforting bubble. The anxiety that once plagued me seemed to melt away, and I felt like I had finally discovered the secret to navigating social interactions with grace. The fuzzy sense of wellbeing it gave me trumped feeling drunk on any level. I'd fallen in love!

But, as is often the case with enchanting tales, reality soon cast its shadow. The substance that promised to liberate me became a grim reminder of the pitfalls of seeking quick fixes.

The thing is, what Kratom has to offer is too good to be true. And my bubble burst rather spectacularly when the euphoria of Kratom quickly morphed into a cycle of dependency that turned my life upside down.

In the thick of addiction to Kratom, I suffered many uncomfortable side effects. Missing a dose of Kratom was like a personal apocalypse.

The initial discomfort gave way to relentless nausea when I didn't dose, a cruel reminder of the grip this powder had on my life.

Headaches had also became a ceaseless assault on my well-being and were sometimes quite debilitating.

My hair falling out was one of the first things that got my attention. While Kratom withdrawals had made me feel terrible, losing my hair was a shock to the system. If your hair has fallen out, don't worry – I include some helpful advice on nutrition for hair-fall in this book.

As the illusion of Kratom faded, I was left with the harsh reality of addiction. I was no longer dosing to enjoy the fuzzy benefits – I was dosing *just to feel normal*.

What had seemed like a simple, natural solution had entangled me in a web of dependence. The discovery that Kratom was actually the cause of my distress was a bitter pill to swallow.

In the pages of this book, you'll find out more about Kratom and what it's effects are. This booked is aimed at Kratom users trying to quit, people considering taking Kratom for the first time, and loved ones of those who are hopelessly addicted.

This book aims to help as many people as possible to see the truth about Kratom and to choose to act against it.

As you turn each page, I hope that you're one step closer to living a Kratom-free life.

# Chapter One
# The Basics

Somewhere in the dense, muggy jungles of Southeast Asia grows a tree that's been giving the locals a buzz for centuries.

This tree, *Mitragyna speciosa*—or Kratom, if you don't fancy chewing through Latin—is no ordinary bit of flora.

It's a cousin of the coffee plant, which explains why both tend to turn human beings into slightly more excitable versions of themselves. But before you start picturing Kratom as a leaf-based espresso, let's clarify: this isn't your morning cup of Joe.

Kratom is a complex plant with a resume that ranges from being a mild pain reliever to making people feel like they don't have a care in the world.

## The Science Bit

At its core, Kratom is basically a leaf with an identity crisis. Chewed fresh by farmers in Thailand or ground into powder for those of us who don't fancy plucking leaves off trees, it contains a variety of alkaloids.

Alkaloids are the chemical compounds responsible for everything from getting you caffeinated to, say, numbing you during surgery (morphine). The two most important alkaloids in Kratom are mitragynine and 7-hydroxymitragynine.

Here's what they do:

- Mitragynine: The principal psychoactive component, this alkaloid has stimulating effects at low doses, meaning it's the one that gives users energy, focus, and the general ability to stop scrolling through TikTok and actually get stuff done.

- 7-hydroxymitragynine: The powerhouse of the plant. This little devil is responsible for the more intense, opioid-like effects. It's also a lot stronger than mitragynine when it comes to pain relief and sedation, which probably explains why it's compared to a mild version of morphine.

Together, these compounds work on the brain's opioid receptors but in a weirdly non-committal way. Unlike actual opioids (think heroin, morphine, and prescription painkillers), Kratom's alkaloids don't fully latch onto the receptors. They just hover around, nudging the receptors, saying, "Hey, calm down a bit, but don't lose your mind." This partial activation is why Kratom users can experience pain relief without the extreme respiratory depression that comes with full-blown opioids.

## How It's Marketed (And Why It's Questionable)

Naturally, when something gives you energy and numbs pain without a prescription, people take notice. So, Kratom has become a bit of a commodity, especially in the West. You can now find it sold in pill form, powder, tea bags, and even gummy bears. Here's where the marketing gets... ambitious.

Kratom is often touted as a natural cure-all, sort of like how aloe vera claims to cure everything from sunburns to heartbreak. Promoters of Kratom will have you believe it's the Chuck Norris of herbal remedies. It can apparently treat just about everything under the sun, and if you let them keep talking, they'll probably tell you it also fixes Wi-Fi connections and gives you perfect pitch.

Here's a non-exhaustive list of what Kratom is said to treat:

- Chronic pain (especially back pain)
- Fatigue
- Anxiety
- Depression
- PTSD
- Insomnia
- Diarrhea
- Opiate withdrawal

Sounds miraculous, right? Like Kratom is the missing ingredient to a life of eternal bliss. But of course, it's not that simple. The reality is, while there are some studies that back up its ability to manage things like pain and opioid withdrawal symptoms, Kratom's overall effects on the human body are still largely a mystery. And, as with all things, side effects exist. We're talking nausea, vomiting, constipation, liver damage, and in some cases, good old-fashioned addiction.

Fun times.

## The Legal Grey Zone

Now, let's talk about Kratom legality. Depending on where you live, Kratom is either the herbal hero of the natural health movement, or a dodgy substance with an asterisk next to it.

In places like Thailand and Malaysia (where it's originally from), Kratom was banned for decades, largely due to concerns about addiction and abuse. In the U.S., it currently sits in the legal grey zone where federal regulators haven't yet decided if it's a friend or foe. Some states and cities have banned it, while in others, you can find Kratom sold openly at gas stations, head shops, and, I assume, from the back of someone's van.

Regulators and scientists remain divided on whether Kratom is a benign herbal remedy or a dangerous, addictive substance.

The Food and Drug Administration (FDA) isn't thrilled about it, and they've repeatedly issued warnings about potential health risks. Meanwhile, Kratom supporters argue that it's a lifesaver for those dealing with chronic pain or opioid addiction, with far fewer side effects than pharmaceutical drugs.

Which side is right? Well, the jury is still very much out on that one.

# Chapter Two
# The Back Story

## (Told Creatively, Of Course)

Picture this: it's 19th-century Southeast Asia. The jungles are thick, sticky with heat, and buzzing with the constant hum of life. And in the middle of it all is a humble farmer, absolutely knackered from a long day of working in the fields.

His hands are blistered, his back feels like it was forged in the pits of Mount Doom, and he's still got three hours of daylight left. What's he to do? Well, if you guessed "pop a few Advil," you're off by a century and several pharmaceutical breakthroughs. But what he does have is something arguably more interesting: a tree, tall and unassuming, with leaves that contain a secret.

This is the Mitragyna speciosa, known to its friends as Kratom.

For hundreds of years, locals in Thailand, Malaysia, and Indonesia had been chewing on these leaves to get a pleasant boost of energy and a surprising reduction in pain. Workers in the fields would munch on the leaves to power through long days, farmers chewed them to dull the aches of manual labor, and occasionally someone would brew it into tea because, well, tea.

## The Accidental Discovery of Kratom's Powers

There wasn't exactly a singular moment where one person "discovered" Kratom like Isaac Newton discovered gravity. Instead, Kratom's powers were stumbled upon by locals who had access to the plant growing all around them.

For centuries, it was the equivalent of coffee and ibuprofen all rolled into one leaf-shaped package. Except with a slight twist: the more Kratom you took, the more the plant's effects changed. Low doses? You're good to go, a pep in your step, like a jungle-caffeinated Superman. But higher doses? Things got a bit more sedate. Pain went away, sure, but so did your general desire to stay awake.

The Southeast Asian laborers weren't scientists, but they didn't have to be. They knew what worked. The Kratom leaf had become the go-to cure for exhaustion, pain, and the general existential dread that comes from spending every waking hour farming in a monsoon. Had a long day? Chew a leaf. Sore back? Have some tea. Want to chill out with your buddies and philosophize about life? Guess what—you're going to want that leaf again.

## Kratom Crosses the Ocean (And Gains a Bit of Baggage)

Now, fast forward to the 1800s. Enter the colonizers, wandering around Southeast Asia, being helpful (by which I mean pillaging everything and drinking tea). During their travels, they noticed that these native workers seemed unnaturally chirpy given the backbreaking labor they were doing.

Some nosy colonizers—who probably hadn't discovered coffee yet—saw the locals chewing on this strange leaf and decided to investigate. Being curious folks, they did what any rational human would do when encountering a strange plant: they tried it for themselves.

And surprise, surprise, they liked it. Kratom wasn't just some local remedy; it was the epitome of herbal goodness. By the time the colonizers got around to telling the folks back home, Kratom had made its way out of the dense forests of Southeast Asia and into the inquisitive minds of European explorers, scientists, and— inevitably—the medical community.

## The 20th Century: The Age of "Oops, This Might Be Addictive"

Fast forward again to the early 1900s, when scientists started poking around with Kratom. They isolated its active compounds—mitragynine and 7-hydroxymitragynine—and quickly realized that this wasn't just a leafy pick-me-up. Kratom had real potential. Pain relief, energy boosting, mood enhancing. The whole package.

But with great alkaloids comes great responsibility. The problem was that the alkaloids in Kratom shared an uncanny resemblance to the chemical structure of opioids.

As more people in the West got their hands on it, scientists began noticing that, while Kratom wasn't as potent as heroin or morphine, it still had the capacity to turn people into leaf addicts. Governments, with their usual nuance and calm, immediately panicked.

By the mid-20th century, Kratom found itself banned in Thailand (ironic, considering it had been a national pastime for centuries). The Thai government wasn't thrilled about farmers using Kratom as an alternative to opium, and this led to one of the most bizarre moments in botanical history: cutting down Kratom trees to prevent drug addiction. Yes, the Thai government thought the best way to fight addiction was to chop down entire forests of Kratom trees. This was essentially the "kill the mosquito with a bazooka" approach.

## Kratom's Revival in the West (Because of Course It Was)

Fast forward again—this time to the early 2000s. While Kratom had been quietly lingering in the background for decades, it was suddenly making a comeback in the West, specifically in the United States. The internet was booming, and with it came online communities, where herbal enthusiasts and people looking for natural pain relief started talking about this mysterious Southeast Asian leaf that had "all the benefits of painkillers, without the nasty side effects". (Spoiler alert: turns out there are side effects, but we'll get to that later.)

Kratom started popping up in head shops, gas stations, and online stores. You could buy it as a powder, in capsules, or even in pre-made tea blends. It was the perfect storm: natural, legal (sort of), and easily accessible. To many, Kratom seemed like the perfect alternative to prescription painkillers, especially in the midst of the opioid crisis. People were desperate for something that wasn't Big Pharma, and Kratom fit the bill.

## How It Became Accessible to Everyone (With a Side of Chaos)

Once the cat was out of the bag, there was no putting it back. Kratom's accessibility exploded. You didn't need to live in Thailand anymore to chew the leaves straight off the tree—you could just hop on Amazon and get a bag of powdered Kratom delivered to your door within 48 hours, along with a yoga mat and some organic kombucha.

The internet and wellness movements latched onto Kratom like it was the latest superfood (move over, kale), and soon enough, it became the new darling of the alternative health world.

But here's the thing: Kratom was still very much in a legal grey zone. The FDA wasn't thrilled about a substance that worked on the brain's opioid receptors being sold at gas stations. The DEA started issuing warnings. Some states outright banned it. But that only made it more desirable, because nothing says "try me" like something almost illegal.

So now, we live in a world where Kratom is both a miracle cure and a potential hazard, depending on who you ask. Some people swear by it for chronic pain, anxiety, or opioid withdrawal. Others are concerned it could be the next addictive disaster waiting to happen. But one thing's for sure: Kratom isn't just a jungle secret anymore. It's a full-blown global product, with all the benefits and risks that come with it.

# Chapter Three
# What People Use Kratom For

Kratom can be used to wake up, calm down, fix your back pain, battle your existential dread, and maybe even impress your in-laws (but don't quote me on that last one).

But before you run off to buy some Kratom from the local head shop, let's be clear about something: people use Kratom for many reasons. And a lot of those reasons make perfect sense... until they don't.

Because here's the thing: behind every "I'm just using it to help with stress" is the tiny, lurking reality that this "miracle plant" can also make you quite dependent.

Let's break the reasons people turn to Kratom.

## 1. Energy

You've been there. It's 3 PM, your productivity is sinking faster than the Titanic, and you've got a mountain of work to do. Coffee? Already had four cups. Energy drink? You're not that desperate yet. So you try Kratom. A little spoonful of the powder, maybe a capsule, and BOOM: you're suddenly working like a god among mortals. You feel focused, clear-headed, and your mood's been perked up.

### What you're thinking

"Hey, this is great! It's like my brain finally found the ON switch!"

## What's actually happening

Your body is enjoying a delightful mix of mitragynine stimulating your opioid receptors, just enough to make you feel like your workload is manageable. You feel invincible, but in reality, your brain is learning to rely on this little boost. So, you use it again. And again. Until one day, you wake up, don't take Kratom, and suddenly realize your brain has no idea how to function without it.

## The slippery slope

You start with a little to "get through the day," but eventually, your body builds tolerance. Now it takes more Kratom to get the same kick. Fast forward a few months: you're using it daily, not because you need energy, but because your brain refuses to work without it.

## 2. Pain

Chronic back pain, migraines, old injuries—whatever the source of your suffering, Kratom comes in like a knight in leafy armor. Pop some Kratom, and suddenly that searing back pain feels like a distant memory. It's like you've taken your own personal morphine shot, but without the pesky side effects or the need for a prescription.

## What you're thinking

"I've found a natural painkiller! Why would I ever need to go back to ibuprofen?"

## What's actually happening

Pain relief feels wonderful. The 7-hydroxymitragynine in Kratom binds to your opioid receptors, much like morphine, taking the edge off your pain. But here's the catch: your body likes this. And your brain really likes this. After a while, it's going to demand the same relief even for the tiniest aches and pains.

## The slippery slope

The more Kratom you take for pain, the more your brain depends on it to feel "normal." At first, it's just to relieve pain. But as tolerance grows, your body needs more of it just to keep things neutral. And soon enough, you're not taking Kratom because you're in pain—you're taking it to avoid withdrawal symptoms like irritability and fatigue.

## 3. Anxiety

You've got a big presentation at work. Or maybe you're just an anxious mess 24/7, thanks to the modern world being a cauldron of stress, expectations, and Twitter fights. You've heard Kratom can help. Just a small dose, and you're calm, relaxed, and somehow able to handle social interactions without wanting to curl up into a ball.

## What you're thinking

"Wow, Kratom takes the edge off my anxiety. I feel so much more in control!"

## What's actually happening

The mild euphoria you're feeling? That's Kratom tapping into those lovely opioid receptors again. It makes everything feel less intense, less stressful. And you like it. Who wouldn't? But here's the catch: after a while, you'll feel more anxious without it. Your brain starts to rely on Kratom to regulate your anxiety levels, meaning the very thing you used to help manage stress can actually increase your anxiety when you're not taking it.

## The slippery slope

You start using Kratom to avoid that jittery, anxious feeling. At first, it's just for special occasions—public speaking, stressful days at work. But soon enough, every day feels stressful, and you're taking Kratom just to keep the baseline anxiety at bay. Without it, you're a nervous wreck.

## 4. Sleep

It's late. You're staring at the ceiling. Sleep is about as close to happening as world peace. Then you remember: Kratom! At high doses, it's a sedative and before you know it, you're drifting off into a peaceful sleep.

## What you're thinking

"This is perfect! It helps me sleep, and I don't need to take Ambien or NyQuil anymore."

## What's actually happening

Sure, Kratom can knock you out like a lullaby, but the more you use it to sleep, the more your body becomes dependent on it. What was once a natural alternative to sleeping pills is now the thing your brain demands to shut down at night.

## The slippery slope

You'll start needing higher doses to fall asleep, and soon you'll find yourself in the cycle of taking Kratom every night just to avoid insomnia. Then the real kicker: when you try to stop, you can't sleep at all. Because your brain is too busy screaming for the thing it's now addicted to.

## 5. Escapism

Life sucks sometimes. Relationships fall apart, work gets stressful, and existential dread sets in like a cloud of bees. Enter Kratom. At higher doses, it's not just about energy or pain relief anymore—it's about escaping reality. You feel euphoric, light, maybe even a little numb to the world's chaos. For a brief moment, everything feels okay.

### What you're thinking

"Kratom helps me forget my problems. I feel so much better after taking it."

### What's actually happening

You're using Kratom as an emotional crutch. Rather than dealing with the stresses of life, you're chemically numbing them. It works—until it doesn't. Because when Kratom wears off, the problems are still there. And now, your brain wants more of that sweet, sweet escape.

### The slippery slope

Soon, you're using Kratom not to feel good, but to stop feeling bad. Life's problems don't go away, but the Kratom does, leaving you in a cycle of dependency that's hard to break out of.

## The Downward Addiction Spiral

No one wakes up one day and thinks, "You know what? I'd like to be addicted to a plant today." But Kratom has a funny way of sneaking up on you. What starts as a seemingly harmless, natural remedy for a real problem—pain, anxiety, insomnia—can quickly turn into a daily crutch. And once you're in the cycle of dependency, your body doesn't care that Kratom is "natural." It just knows that without it, things feel terrible.

## How to Tell If Someone's Hooked on Kratom of If Your Addiction Has Gone Too Far

How do you know if someone is using Kratom? It's not like they'll be walking around with a neon sign over their head saying, "I've just downed some Southeast Asian plant powder." And how do you know if your use of Kratom has gone to too far? When someone is using Kratom more than they should, a few tell-tale signs start to emerge.

Let's take a look at some of the classic symptoms, the warning signs that someone in your life (or even you) might be slipping into Kratom dependency. And since I believe in making this as personal as possible, let's sprinkle in a few stories from my own life, because, believe me, I've seen these signs up close—and lived to tell the tale.

## Irritability: When Everything Becomes a Battle Royale

One of the first signs that someone's using Kratom, especially when they're coming down from a dose or starting to crave another one, is good ol' fashioned *irritability.* You know the type—someone who turns into a ticking time bomb, just waiting for you to say the wrong thing, like "What do you want for dinner?" or "Did you remember to pay that bill?"

I'll admit it: I've been that person. When I was using Kratom regularly, I could go from zero to absolutely ballistic in a matter of seconds. My ex-boyfriend can definitely attest to that. He used to make these offhand comments, like suggesting I take a break from work or that we should maybe "talk about our feelings more." And there I was, snapping like a rubber band, yelling about how *he didn't understand* or how *he was always criticizing me.* In retrospect, it was like living in a permanent emotional minefield, where every little thing felt like an attack.

Kratom messes with your emotional regulation. You're calm and relaxed when it's flowing through your system, but the second that balance tips, irritability kicks in hard. Your fuse gets shorter, and suddenly, everything feels like an argument waiting to happen. If you've noticed someone in your life going from mellow to monstrous in the blink of an eye, Kratom might be part of the equation.

## Mood Swings: From Chill to Chaotic Faster Than You Can Say "Tea"

Hand in hand with irritability are the *mood swings.* One minute, the person is the chillest human being you've ever met, practically oozing relaxation like they've just spent an hour in a hot yoga class. The next, they're spiraling into frustration or sadness, like they've been slapped by the universe itself.

The emotional rollercoaster of Kratom use isn't just annoying—it's exhausting for everyone involved. When I was deep in it, I'd have days where I felt like I was in total control of my life, and then BAM, out of nowhere, the come-down hit me like a freight train. Cue the sadness, the self-doubt, and the sudden feeling that everything was hopeless. I remember one particular evening after I'd had some Kratom (and mixed it with a few glasses of wine—more on that disaster later), when I went from laughing hysterically at a comedy special on Netflix to crying on the kitchen floor because the pasta I was making didn't "feel right."

Yeah. You read that correctly.

Mood swings like that aren't normal, and they're one of the clearest signs that someone's using something that's messing with their internal chemistry, especially when mixing it with alcohol. If someone you know seems to be all over the place emotionally—serene one moment and totally frazzled the next—it might be worth considering if Kratom is playing a role in that chaos.

## Fatigue: The Walking Zombie Effect

Here's another fun one: *fatigue*. While Kratom can give you a boost in small doses, in higher doses or with prolonged use, it does the opposite. You end up feeling sluggish, tired, and like every limb is weighed down with lead. You'd think that after taking something that's supposed to *help* with energy, you wouldn't be dragging yourself around like an extra in a zombie movie, but alas, that's exactly what happens.

I vividly remember the phase where I could barely drag myself out of bed in the mornings. It didn't matter how much Kratom I'd had the day before or how "energizing" it was supposed to be—by the time it wore off, I felt like I'd run a marathon in my sleep. There was one morning where I slept through three alarms, missed an important work call, and woke up in such a haze that it took me a full five minutes to even remember what day it was. Not exactly my finest moment.

The thing with Kratom is that while it might give you a temporary lift, it also messes with your sleep cycle and overall energy levels. Over time, this fatigue becomes harder to shake, and before you know it, you're stuck in this permanent state of exhaustion, chasing that next dose just to feel normal again.

## Loss of Appetite: When Even Pizza Loses Its Appeal

Now, let's talk about *loss of appetite*, because nothing says "something's wrong" like someone turning down a slice of pizza. Kratom can mess with your hunger cues, and after a while, food just stops being a priority. You'd rather sit around feeling slightly queasy than eat a meal, and that, my friends, is a red flag the size of a house.

During my Kratom days, I had whole stretches of time where I basically forgot food existed. I'd go for hours without eating, not because I was consciously trying to lose weight or anything, but because I just wasn't hungry. My ex-boyfriend would bring home dinner, and I'd take a few bites before pushing the plate away, complaining that I "just didn't feel like it." This, coming from someone who once described pizza as "the love of my life."

Kratom can dull your hunger in the same way it dulls your emotions. There's also the little fact that it works better on an empty stomach, so some of the "not hungry" can be all in your head. Eventually, people start to notice the weight loss, the pale complexion, the general disinterest in food. If someone in your life is suddenly skipping meals or losing weight without explanation, and they seem to be carrying around that trademark Kratom powder in their bag, it's probably not a coincidence.

## Mixing Kratom and Alcohol: A One-Way Ticket to Disaster

If I had to choose a single moment when I knew Kratom had gone too far, it would be the night I thought mixing it with alcohol was a brilliant idea.

You see, Kratom and alcohol don't play nicely together. Kratom's sedative effects can amplify when mixed with booze, and what starts as a relaxing evening can turn into a full-blown blackout faster than you can say "bad decisions." I should know—one night, after downing a few glasses of wine, I thought it would be "fun" to have some Kratom to mellow out.

That night ended with me lying on the bathroom floor, dizzy, nauseous, and desperately trying to remember how many glasses I'd had. The next morning was even worse. It wasn't just a hangover—it was like my brain had been replaced with a concrete block. My emotions were shot, my body felt like it had been run over, and I spent the entire day swearing I'd never do that again.

Mixing alcohol and Kratom is dangerous. It intensifies the side effects of both substances, leading to confusion, extreme drowsiness, and in some cases, blackouts. If someone you know is using Kratom and drinking on top of it, that's a huge red flag. Trust me—nothing good comes from combining the two.

**Withdrawal Symptoms: The Biggest Give-Away of All**

Finally, we come to the biggest tell-tale sign of all: *withdrawal symptoms*. When someone's using Kratom regularly, and then they stop or cut back, the withdrawal kicks in, and it's not pretty. We're talking about anxiety, nausea, sweating, irritability, and general misery that makes them wish they could just curl up in a ball and disappear.

I remember one particularly awful weekend when I decided to quit cold turkey (bad idea, by the way). By Sunday, I was sweating through my sheets, my legs were twitching uncontrollably, and my anxiety was through the roof. I snapped at everyone, cried for no reason, and generally felt like a mess. It wasn't just physical—it was mental too. The cravings were intense, and all I could think about was how much better I'd feel if I just had one more dose. That's how you know something's got its hooks in you.

If someone's showing signs of withdrawal—sudden mood swings, irritability, physical discomfort—and they've been using Kratom, chances are they're in deeper than they want to admit.

# Chapter Four
# The Nasty Side Effects

When my relationship ended with Kratom, I'd come to see it as the shady cousin of caffeine who shows up to family gatherings uninvited, wrecks the house, and then steals your wallet.

The nasty side effects and dangers of taking Kratom should be enough to get most people quitting, but the addiction is often just too powerful.

## 1. Addiction: Welcome to Your New Full-Time Job

People love to say Kratom isn't addictive because it's a plant, as if nature somehow guarantees safety. That's like saying "this snake won't kill you because it's from the jungle." Newsflash: lots of things from nature will ruin your life. Kratom just happens to be one of them.

See, when you take Kratom, especially in larger doses, it binds to opioid receptors in your brain—the same ones that make heroin and morphine so darn charming. Except Kratom sneaks in through the back door, disguised as a "herbal remedy," and before you know it, you're stuck in a cycle. A dependency forms, and you're now spending your days chasing the next dose like a caffeine addict running after their third venti latte.

The withdrawal symptoms are a delightful buffet of nausea, sweating, muscle aches, irritability, and, my personal favorite, the feeling that your skin might crawl off your body and find a new host.

## 2. Respiratory Depression: Because Breathing is Optional, Apparently

You know that thing your body does, where it automatically breathes for you? Yeah, Kratom doesn't like that. In high doses, it can cause respiratory depression, which is science talk for, "Your brain forgets how to breathe." And in case you missed the memo, breathing is sort of important. It's the kind of function you really want your body to keep up with, even when you're not paying attention.

Kratom's opioid-like properties can suppress the central nervous system, slowing down all the important stuff: heart rate, lung function, and the part of your brain that should be reminding you not to die. If you're already mixing it with other downers (like alcohol or, I don't know, actual opioids), congratulations—you've just signed up for the slow suffocation express. Please remain seated while your ability to breathe diminishes one puff at a time.

## 3. Liver Toxicity: Or How to Kill Your Liver Without the Fun of a Boozy Weekend

Ah, the liver—our poor, overworked detox machine. It's the organ that gets the short end of the stick every time we decide to indulge in questionable substances, and Kratom is no exception.

One of the charming little side effects of prolonged Kratom use is liver toxicity. Your favorite plant-based "cure" can make your liver wave the white flag and say,

"I'm out." Over time, Kratom can lead to cholestatic liver injury, which is basically your liver's way of telling you it's tired of processing your bad decisions. Symptoms include yellowing of the skin and eyes (that's called jaundice), dark urine, and itchy skin. So, while you're chasing your Kratom high, your liver's quietly breaking down, piece by piece, like the old computer in the back of your closet that crashes every time you try to open Microsoft Word. By the time you realize your liver's gone rogue, it might be too late to fix the damage.

## 4. Psychosis: When Reality Starts to Feel a Bit... Optional

Kratom can send your brain off the deep end. Long-term use has been linked to psychosis, which is a fancy way of saying that your grip on reality starts to slip. Hallucinations, delusions, paranoia—it's the full "walking through a funhouse mirror" experience, except it's happening inside your head, and there's no exit sign.

Think about it: you're just trying to get through the day, maybe relax after a hard week, and suddenly, you're convinced your neighbor is plotting to steal your identity. Or worse, you see things that aren't there—shadowy figures out of the corner of your eye, voices whispering your name.

## 5. Seizures: When Your Brain Decides to Take a Quick Break

Speaking of your brain malfunctioning, let's talk about *seizures*. Because what's better than having your day interrupted by your brain deciding to have an unscheduled electrical storm? Nothing quite says "I've made a great life choice" like seizing uncontrollably on your kitchen floor after trying to self-medicate with Kratom.

There's evidence that high doses of Kratom can lower the seizure threshold, making it easier for your brain to short-circuit. This is especially true if you're someone with a history of seizures or, once again, if you enjoy mixing Kratom with other substances like a mad scientist who has a death wish. So, in addition to potential respiratory failure, liver damage, and a psychotic break, you now also have to worry about your brain deciding it's time for an impromptu dance party.

## 6. Gastrointestinal Delight: Vomiting and Constipation, Together at Last

Kratom has this unique ability to cause both vomiting and constipation, which is a delightful combination when you really think about it. Imagine being unable to keep food down while simultaneously being unable to get it out. Fun, right?

In small doses, Kratom might give you mild nausea or a bit of stomach discomfort. But when you start ramping up the dosage—because, let's be real, once you start, you're not going to stop—your body responds by flipping the "evacuate all contents" switch. You'll find yourself becoming intimately familiar with your toilet bowl, wondering why this plant that was supposed to relax you is now making you feel like you've contracted the stomach flu.

On the flip side, the same plant that's got you puking your guts out can also block your bowels.

## 7. Death: The Final Side Effect

If the psychosis, liver damage, respiratory failure, and seizures weren't enough to deter you, there's always the possibility that Kratom might just kill you outright.

There have been several reports of Kratom-related deaths, often involving people who took Kratom along with other substances, but sometimes all on its own. And while dying might sound like the ultimate escape from your responsibilities, I can't imagine Kratom is the kind of ride you want to take to get there. It's not good for you or the people who love you.

## 8. Hair Loss: Because Bald is the New You

If you thought Kratom was just going to mess with your internal organs and your brain, buckle up, because it's coming for your *hair* too. Kratom has been linked to *hair loss*.

Long-term Kratom use can mess with your body's hormonal balance. And when your hormones go haywire, your hairline starts making a quiet exit, leaving you looking in the mirror wondering why the top of your head is suddenly getting so much air time.

If you've ever wanted to try out wigs, now's your chance! Though I suppose you could always blame the stress at work for your sudden thinning hair—except, of course, it's not the job. It's the plant that was supposed to help you *deal* with the job.

To be fair, Kratom doesn't seem to be as effective as, say, male pattern baldness, but give it enough time and doses, and you might just find yourself calling it quits on hair products altogether.

## 9. Loss of Appetite: When You're Just Too High to Eat

Kratom's not just here to take your hair. It also wants to make sure you lose a few pounds in the process. Now, I know what you're thinking: "Isn't weight loss a *good* thing?" Maybe, but not like this. Kratom-induced *loss of appetite* isn't about shedding a few pounds to fit into your summer clothes. It's about your body straight-up rejecting the idea of food altogether.

Imagine feeling a combination of nauseated and disinterested in eating anything beyond a cracker or a spoonful of yogurt. Sounds fun, right? You're basically turning into a zombie who can't even work up the enthusiasm to munch on brains. Kratom dulls your hunger cues, making food seem like a chore rather than a basic necessity. What's the point of pizza if Kratom's convinced your stomach it's *too much effort* to digest?

Over time, you might even start looking a little gaunt, as if you've just returned from a retreat to the middle of nowhere, where they fed you nothing but fresh air and bad vibes. Friends will ask if you're "doing okay" or "trying out a new diet," and you'll smile awkwardly while fighting the urge to throw up the three spoonfuls of cereal you managed to force down that morning.

Loss of appetite can lead to some serious nutritional deficiencies, and let's be real, malnutrition isn't a good look. So, while Kratom might make your jeans a little looser, it's not exactly the health plan you signed up for. Fewer calories? Sure. But also fewer vitamins, fewer minerals, and a body running on fumes.

# Chapter Five
# The Many Ways People Take Kratom

When I first started taking Kratom, I discovered that there's a whole buffet of ways to get Kratom into your system. Here's a few of them:

## 1. Toss and Wash

This is the method where you literally take a spoonful of Kratom powder—yes, a big, green, clumpy pile of powder that looks like it was scraped out of a lawnmower—and toss it directly into your mouth.

Then, because your body immediately regrets all your life decisions, you frantically wash it down with a glass of water, juice, or whatever liquid is closest, trying not to gag as the Kratom swirls in your mouth like the world's worst protein shake.

The genius behind toss and wash is that it's fast. You're skipping all the pleasantries of actually preparing the stuff. Just scoop, toss, chug, and pray you don't accidentally inhale it.

## 2. Capsules

Next up, we have capsules, the option for those who want to experience Kratom without the taste and texture of dirt-flavored sludge. You know the drill: Kratom gets stuffed into capsules, you pop a few (or a few dozen, because let's be real, you need a lot of Kratom to feel anything), and then you wait for the magic to happen.

Capsules are for the kind of people who would rather lie to themselves. "Oh, look at me! I'm taking a nice, neat little pill, like a responsible adult. Surely this is healthy." Spoiler alert: it's still Kratom. You're still consuming a substance that could make your liver wave the white flag. But hey, at least it looks like you're just downing some organic fish oil, so that's something.

The downside to capsules is that you need to take approximately 57 of them to get the same effect as a teaspoon of powder. Okay, maybe that's an exaggeration, but you get the point. You'll be sitting there for a solid five minutes, swallowing capsule after capsule like a human Tic-Tac dispenser, wondering why the hell you didn't just go for the toss and wash method and get it over with.

## 3. Kratom Tea

Now, for the sophisticated among us, there's Kratom tea. This is for those who want to feel like they're part of some ancient herbal ritual, even though you're really just steeping a bunch of questionable green powder in hot water and pretending it's chai.

Making Kratom tea involves brewing the powder or crushed leaves (yes, crushed leaves if you're really feeling rustic) in boiling water, straining out the plant material, and sipping on the murky liquid like you're drinking some exotic potion.

The upside of Kratom tea is that it's a more pleasant way to ingest the stuff compared to shoveling powder into your mouth. The downside is, well, the taste. No amount of honey or sugar is going to turn this into a cozy beverage experience. You'll take one sip, immediately regret it, but then keep going because hey, you've already committed.

And let's not forget the brewing process itself. Trying to steep Kratom is like performing a dark art. Too little heat, and you've got a lukewarm swamp drink. Too much heat, and you've destroyed the alkaloids, which is the only reason you're drinking this abomination in the first place. It's like brewing tea for someone you hate, except the person you hate is yourself.

## 4. Kratom Smoothies

With this method, you take some Kratom powder, throw it into your overpriced blender, add a bunch of fruit, maybe some spinach (because health), and then blend it all into a green sludge that looks like something a swamp monster might drink.

In your mind, you're a health guru, mixing the best of nature into one powerhouse beverage. In reality, you're choking down Kratom-flavored mush and wondering if the antioxidants from the blueberries will cancel out the slow organ damage the Kratom's doing.

The worst part? Kratom doesn't blend well. You'll be sipping your smoothie, trying to convince yourself it's palatable, only to be smacked in the face by a clump of unmixed Kratom powder halfway through. And let me tell you, nothing ruins a morning quite like chewing on a chunk of what feels like dirt mixed with despair.

## 5. Kratom Extracts

Now, for the hardcore among us, there are Kratom extracts. This is when you take all the fun, messy parts of

Kratom—the leaves, the powder—and distill it down into a concentrated liquid or resin that's supposed to be stronger, faster, better. Basically, the "I want to feel something NOW" version of Kratom.

You can drop it under your tongue like it's some kind of edgy herbal tincture, or mix it into your tea if you really want to spice up your day. Either way, the result is the same: a faster, more intense Kratom experience, and an even higher likelihood of regret.

The thing with extracts is that you're playing with fire. Regular Kratom's already a slippery slope, but the extract? It's like throwing yourself off the edge and hoping you land in a pool of good life decisions (spoiler: you won't). Sure, you'll get your Kratom kick quicker, but you'll also get the side effects faster. Nausea, dizziness, that creeping feeling of, "Oh God, what have I done," all packed into a neat little bottle.

Extracts are for the people who've graduated from the "mild interest in Kratom" phase and are now deep into the "I may have made a terrible life choice, but it's too late to stop now" phase.

## 6. Kratom Edibles

Kratom edibles come in many forms: gummies, chocolates, and even baked goods, for the adventurous souls who want their Kratom to come with a side of dessert. You can take your Kratom, mix it into a batch of cookies, and voilà!

The problem, of course, is that edibles are sneaky. You eat one gummy, think, "Huh, I don't feel anything," and then proceed to eat three more. Two hours later, you're lying on your couch wondering why your liver feels like it's auditioning for Cirque du Soleil. And because it's food, you're left with that classic conundrum of "should I eat more to balance out the weirdness?" (Answer: No. Always no.)

## 7. Topical Kratom

I discovered that there are out here rubbing Kratom-infused creams and lotions onto their skin in the hopes of getting some pain relief or anti-inflammatory benefits. You know, because ingesting Kratom wasn't enough, we now have to slather it on like we're getting ready for a weird spa day.

The idea behind topical Kratom is that it can be absorbed through the skin, providing localized relief without the whole "ingesting something potentially harmful" thing. Except, of course, it's still Kratom, and your skin is still absorbing it, and this entire method feels like someone lost a bet.

# Chapter Six
# Kratom Dosing

Here's the thing about kratom: dosing it is a bit like trying to parallel park a bus in a tight spot while blindfolded. You don't want too much (unless you enjoy nausea and vomiting), but too little will leave you wondering why you bothered at all. So, how much Kratom should you take? And more importantly, how the hell do people figure out a dosing schedule?

## 1. The Low Dose: The Toe-Dipper's Delight

This is where people ease into their Kratom use.

A low dose of kratom generally falls between 1 and 2 grams of powder. At this level, you'll probably feel a mild boost of energy, maybe a slight increase in focus, and—if you're really lucky—a general sense of well-being. You know, the kind of mild euphoria that makes you think, "Hey, maybe today won't be terrible after all." It's like drinking a strong cup of coffee with an extra kick.

This low-dose effect is what a lot of people are after when they start using kratom. They want the energy boost without all the weirdness that comes with higher doses. It's like taking a polite sip of the kratom cocktail, nodding your head, and saying, "Ah yes, I see why people like this."

## Example Dosing Schedule for Low-Dose Users

- Day 1: 1 gram in the morning to see what happens.

- Day 2: 1.5 grams because you think you can handle more and maybe that was a mistake.
- Day 3: 1 gram again to play it safe after Day 2's mild nausea episode.
- Day 4: Skip kratom.

The low-dose approach is ideal for people who still have a vague sense of self-preservation. It's for the ones who just want a little pep in their step without turning their life into an unpredictable roller coaster.


## 2. The Medium Dose: The Curious-but-Worried Wanderer

So, you've tried the low dose, you're feeling pretty good about yourself, and now you're thinking, "What if I just... take a little more?" Well, congratulations, you've entered the medium dose range, aka the land of curious wanderers who haven't yet learned the meaning of restraint.

A medium dose falls between 3 and 5 grams of kratom powder.
At this point, you're not just looking for a bit of energy anymore—you're looking for something more... significant. Something that might make you feel like you've discovered the secret to inner peace (or, at the very least, to sitting still for longer than 15 minutes without existential dread creeping in).

At 3-5 grams, kratom starts to take on a different character. It's still stimulating, but there's a subtle shift toward relaxation. You're no longer just energized—you're chill. You're vibing, as the kids would say. Sure, your body feels good, but you're also wondering whether maybe you're a bit too relaxed to function.

## Example Dosing Schedule for Medium-Dose Enthusiasts

- Day 1: 3 grams in the afternoon, because why not skip the low-dose phase and get to the good stuff?
- Day 2: 4 grams in the evening because you want to see if the "chill factor" really kicks in.
- Day 3: 3 grams mid-morning, and now you're second-guessing whether kratom at breakfast was a solid life choice.
- Day 4: 5 grams, because YOLO, and now you're lying on the couch contemplating the nature of reality while wondering if you've become a sentient beanbag.

At medium doses, you've entered the realm of experimentation. You're still mostly in control, but your body's starting to ask some questions. And the answer is always, "More? Maybe more?"

## 3. The High Dose: The Bold Adventurer on the Brink

This is for people who have thrown caution to the wind, along with any semblance of moderation. You've decided that you want to feel something, and you don't particularly care if that feeling is blissful euphoria or intense nausea. At this level, you're dancing with the devil and hoping he's got good moves.

A high dose of kratom is anything between 6 and 8 grams, and let me tell you, this is where things get... interesting. You're not just relaxing at this point—you're floating. You're drifting off into a world where your body is so relaxed that it's basically decided to temporarily retire from its responsibilities. Your limbs feel heavy, your mind feels like it's been wrapped in a warm blanket, and you're either about to have the best nap of your life or the worst stomachache in recent memory. The problem is that eventually this floaty feeling is no longer achievable, and you'll just be taking the powder to feel some semblance of normal.

At high doses, kratom's sedative effects really kick in. You're no longer energetic—you're sinking into the nearest piece of furniture and becoming one with it. This is also where the side effects start to rear their ugly heads: nausea, dizziness, and that oh-so-wonderful sense of impending doom that accompanies taking too much of something you barely understand.

## Example Dosing Schedule for High-Dose Enthusiasts

- Day 1: 6 grams at noon because you heard from someone on Reddit that this is the "sweet spot."
- Day 2: 7 grams because Day 1 didn't hit quite hard enough, and now you're determined to find out where the line is.
- Day 3: 8 grams. You're feeling nauseous but also profoundly relaxed, and you're wondering whether Kratom is worth the sudden wave of dread.
- Day 4: No kratom, because your body is screaming for a break. Water. Lots of water.

At this point, you're not just playing with fire—you're practically roasting marshmallows over it. High doses are for people who've gone beyond curiosity and are now conducting full-blown science experiments on their own tolerance for suffering.

## 4. The Mega Dose: The "I Have No Self-Control" Award Winner

This is the territory of 9 grams and up, where you've decided to throw logic and reason out the window and take the "more is more" approach to life.

At doses this high, you're not even trying to have a nice time anymore. You're actively pursuing the dark side of kratom, where sedation becomes a state of near-comatose relaxation and nausea becomes a permanent house guest. Your body is no longer vibing; it's writing its will and preparing for the end.

This is where the opioid-like effects really take over, and you'll be lucky if you can stand up without feeling like your legs are made of jello. Spoiler: they probably are, at least metaphorically. Your mind is foggy, your limbs are heavy, and you've reached a point of detachment from reality that might as well come with a warning label. And when you start a day without kratom, you'll feel unbalanced and dizzy – thus your body is demanding its usual treat!

### Example Dosing Schedule for Mega-Dose Daredevils
- Day 1: 9 grams, because why not push the envelope? You're not even sure where you are anymore.
- Day 2: 10 grams. You're reclining in a chair that's slowly becoming your entire existence, and it's questionable whether you'll get up again.
- Day 3: 12 grams. You're lying flat on the floor, unsure of how you got there, but everything's very, very calm.
- Day 4: No kratom. Your organs are pleading for mercy, and you're seriously considering life choices.

---

## The Kratom Dosing Roller Coaster

At the end of the day, dosing kratom is less of a science and more of an art. It's about finding that delicate balance between "this feels nice" and "oh dear God, why is everything spinning?" And that's how so many people become inadvertently addicted.

Sure, you might start with low doses and think you've got it all figured out but give it time. Kratom has a way of making people feel invincible, right up until the moment they're lying on the bathroom floor, questioning their existence.

# Chapter Seven
# How to Quit Kratom

**Disclaimer: I never recommend quitting a substance you're highly addicted to without consulting with a health or medical professional. This information is not a strict guide and is based on my personal experience. It is not meant to replace the advice and guidance of a medical professional**

While I love to take a fun approach to everything, there was truly nothing fun about being addicted to Kratom. I thought I was solving my social drinking problem but very quickly, Kratom consumed me. I became its slave. I wasn't even enjoying social occasions in the end, but I was using them as an excuse to take Kratom.

I was stuck in a vicious cycle I couldn't get out of. I'd lost 10kg of weight, my hair had thinned dramatically, I had black bags under my eyes, I was constantly on edge, and I was starting to lash out in frustration and anger at the most inopportune times. I'd hit rock bottom and I decided I needed to quit. I was tired of being a slave.

You may have different reasons for quitting Kratom (or wanting a loved one to quit). Maybe it's because your liver's staging a coup, or perhaps your significant other is tired of watching you toss back a mountain of green powder every morning like a sad health influencer who gave up on kale. Whatever the reason, it's not going to be a walk in the park.

Quitting Kratom is like breaking up with someone who won't stop texting you at 2 a.m. to remind you of all the good times you had together. It's clingy, annoying, and it's going to test your willpower more than you ever thought possible. I've put together some options for you to consider in the process of evicting Kratom from your life.

## 1. Cold Turkey: The "I'm Tougher Than This Stupid Plant" Method

I find this somewhat of a classic approach. This is the method for people who wake up one morning and think, "You know what? I'm done. No more Kratom. I don't need a crutch, I'm a strong, independent person who can handle anything."

This is undoubtedly the most difficult method but very effective.

If you've been taking Kratom regularly, your body has probably developed a cozy relationship with it. Quitting abruptly is like pulling the rug out from under your nervous system, and your body will react accordingly. Symptoms? Oh, just your standard withdrawal fare: muscle aches, nausea, diarrhea, insomnia, and—everyone's favorite—restless leg syndrome. Picture yourself tossing and turning all night, while your legs do the cha-cha against your will. It's not pretty, but at least you're burning calories, right?

**Effectiveness:** High, if you push through the first few days without crawling back to your stash.

**Comfort level:** Somewhere between a hangover and the worst flu of your life, multiplied by ten.

**Pro tip:** Stock up on blankets, tea, and excuses for why you look like you've just seen a ghost for the next week.

## 2. Tapering Off: The "Let's Take This Slowly" Approach

For those of you who want to take the breakup a little slower, there's tapering off, which is basically the method for people who want to quit without feeling the symptoms too dramatically.

Tapering involves gradually reducing your Kratom intake over the course of weeks (or even months, if you've really been on the Kratom train). Instead of going from 8 grams to 0 overnight, you'll cut back slowly, letting your body adjust to life without constant alkaloid bombardment.

One day you're taking 7 grams, then 6, then 5, until eventually you're down to nothing but the fond memory of your time as a green powder connoisseur.

This method has one major benefit: it doesn't make you feel like death is looming around every corner. You'll still experience some withdrawal symptoms, but they'll be way less intense than the cold turkey approach. Think of it as weaning yourself off Kratom, one small step at a time, like a cautious explorer tiptoeing away from a dangerous volcano.

**Effectiveness:** Very high, as long as you stay disciplined and don't use "tapering" as an excuse to just take less Kratom forever.

**Comfort level:** Manageable. You'll still feel weird, but not "I want to die" levels of weird. You may have headaches, dizziness and nausea.

**Pro tip:** Keep a dosing schedule and stick to it like your life depends on it, because your brain will absolutely try to convince you that one extra gram won't hurt.

### 3. Switching to Another Substance: The "Jump From One Train to Another" Plan

Ah yes, the classic switcheroo. This method involves quitting Kratom by substituting it with something else that's supposed to be easier to quit. It's the psychological equivalent of dumping your current toxic partner by immediately dating someone else who's just as bad, but in different ways.

People who try this method often switch to milder substances like CBD or Kava, hoping that these will give them the same calm, relaxed feeling without the whole "opiate-like withdrawal" situation. On paper, this sounds great. Replace the bad stuff with the not-as-bad stuff, right? But in practice, it's more like playing whack-a-mole with your body's dependency issues.

Sure, CBD might help take the edge off your anxiety or restlessness, but it's not going to fully replace the euphoric, cozy feeling Kratom used to give you. Same with Kava—it might relax your muscles, but it won't save you from the mental fog and cravings that come with quitting. Plus, there's the very real danger of just becoming addicted to your new substance of choice. You're not really quitting; you're just swapping out one problem for another and hoping no one notices.

**Effectiveness:** Medium, depending on what you're switching to and how well you can resist the urge to start using both substances.

**Comfort level:** Variable. You might feel fine, or you might end up with two dependencies instead of one.

**Pro tip:** If you're going to try this, make sure your replacement isn't another form of self-sabotage. You're trying to quit Kratom, not build a buffet of herbal vices.

I personally don't recommend switching to another substance.

## 4. Going to Rehab: The "I've Hit Rock Bottom" Solution

If your Kratom use has gone from casual experimentation to full-blown dependency, and you're lying in bed every night wondering if you're going to wake up feeling like death, it might be time to consider the big guns: rehab.

Rehab is for people who've realized that quitting on their own just isn't going to cut it. Maybe you've tried cold turkey, and your body rebelled so hard you thought you were going to ascend to another dimension. Maybe you've been tapering for months and still can't get below 4 grams without turning into a jittery mess. Or maybe you've just had enough of your Kratom habit dictating every part of your life, and it's time to bring in the professionals.

Rehab provides structure, support, and medical supervision to help you detox from Kratom without feeling like your organs are slowly dissolving. You'll get counseling, therapy, and possibly some helpful medication to ease the worst of the withdrawal symptoms. And the best part? You're surrounded by people who actually know what they're doing, instead of frantically Googling "how to quit Kratom without dying" at 3 a.m.

**Effectiveness:** Extremely high, assuming you're committed to the process and don't run for the door halfway through.

**Comfort level:** Relatively high, especially since you'll be monitored by medical professionals. But make no mistake—it's still detox, and detox is never a good time.

**Pro tip:** If you're in deep, don't be afraid to ask for help. There's no shame in calling in the pros when Kratom has turned into an unwanted houseguest who won't leave.

## 5. Support Groups: The "Let's Do This Together" Method

If you're the kind of person who likes to talk about your feelings (or at least listen to other people's horror stories), then support groups*might be your best option for quitting Kratom. Much like how AA helps alcoholics, there are communities of people who have been through the Kratom trenches and are now on the other side—or at least trying to be.

Support groups provide a space for people to share their experiences, offer tips, and generally remind each other that they're not alone in this mess. It's a solid option if you need accountability and motivation, because trust me, quitting something like Kratom is 100 times harder when you're trying to do it in isolation. And no, your cat doesn't count as a support system, even if it gives you judgmental looks every time you brew another Kratom tea.

**Effectiveness:** High, if you're into talking things out and need that sense of community to stay on track.

**Comfort level:** Depends on how much you enjoy sharing your struggles with a group of strangers. It can be cathartic, or it can be uncomfortable as hell.

**Pro tip:** Find a group that actually understands Kratom. Showing up to a general support group full of people addicted to alcohol or opioids might not get you the best advice, unless you're ready for a bunch of raised eyebrows when you try to explain what Kratom is.

# Chapter Eight
# Studies

Kratom hasn't exactly been studied like, say, chocolate or coffee, which is probably why it's been floating around the fringes of "herbal remedies" for so long. But that doesn't mean scientists haven't poked it with a few beakers. In fact, there's some fascinating stuff out there about this plant—if by fascinating, you mean mildly horrifying and definitely a reason to rethink your tea habits.

## 1. Kratom and Its Alkaloids: The Chemical Nightmare

Kratom contains two major alkaloids that have been the center of attention in most scientific studies—mitragynine and 7-hydroxymitragynine. These bad boys are what give Kratom its opioid-like effects, even though Kratom itself isn't technically classified as an opioid. Think of it like a diet opioid: it's trying to do the same thing, but with less finesse.

In a 2014 study published in the Journal of Ethnopharmacology, researchers took a close look at mitragynine and 7-hydroxymitragynine. What they found was... well, concerning. These compounds bind to the same receptors in the brain that opioids do, which is why Kratom can make you feel pain relief, euphoria, or just an overall sense that maybe life isn't as terrible as you thought. The downside? It also means Kratom has the potential for addiction and withdrawal, just like traditional opioids. You know, the stuff that ruined the 2000s for a lot of people.

This means that while you're sipping on your Kratom tea thinking you've found a safe, natural alternative to pharmaceuticals, your brain is quietly going, "Hey, this feels a lot like those really addictive things we've been warned about." So maybe ease up on the heroic doses of Kratom.

Link:
https://www.sciencedirect.com/search?qs=Mitragynine%20alkaloid%20effects%20Kratom%202014%20Journal%20of%20Ethnopharmacology

## 2. Kratom and Liver Damage: That's Gonna Hurt in the Morning

If you like your liver and would prefer to keep it functioning past your 40s, you're going to want to pay attention to this one.

In a 2020 study published in the Journal of Medical Toxicology, researchers dug into cases of liver injury associated with Kratom use. Spoiler alert: the results weren't great. The study looked at several cases of people who had developed liver damage after using Kratom for a few weeks to a few months. Symptoms included jaundice (you know that fun yellowing of the skin that makes you look like a Simpsons character), fatigue, and—wait for it—elevated liver enzymes. For those playing along at home, that's your liver's way of screaming, "I'm working way too hard, and I need a vacation."

To make matters worse, it turns out that in most of these cases, liver damage popped up even when people weren't using super high doses of Kratom. So, if you were thinking you could avoid liver trouble by just "microdosing," think again. The liver is like a bouncer at a nightclub—eventually, it's going to stop letting the riff-raff in.

Kratom and your liver are not friends. If your pee starts to look like iced tea and your eyes take on a yellowish hue, it's time to rethink that Kratom habit before your liver throws in the towel.

Link: https://link.springer.com/article/10.1007/s40265-019-01242-6

## 3. Kratom and Addiction: The Plant That Won't Let Go

One of the most debated questions in Kratom circles is, "*Is Kratom addictive?*" Well, according to science: yes. Yes, it is.

A study published in Drug and Alcohol Dependence in 2017 focused on Kratom's potential for addiction. It found that people who used Kratom regularly (surprise, surprise) started to develop tolerance and, eventually, withdrawal symptoms when they tried to stop. Symptoms of Kratom withdrawal? You guessed it—restlessness, muscle aches, insomnia, and a lovely thing called runny nose. It's like the flu, but with an extra layer of existential dread thrown in.

In case you were hoping that the addiction potential was mild, the study also mentioned that some people were using up to 100 grams of Kratom per day. Just for context, that's about the same weight as a full-grown hamster. Imagine downing a hamster-sized amount of plant powder every day and then trying to quit cold turkey. Yeah, good luck with that.

Kratom can definitely be addictive, especially if you're using it regularly. So if you think you're immune to dependency because it's "just a plant," think again. Your brain doesn't care where the chemicals come from—it just wants more.

Link: https://ww2.uthscsa.edu/artt/addictionjc/smithandlawson2017.pdf

## 4. Kratom and Death: The Final Side Effect

Now, let's talk about the big one—death. There's been a lot of debate over whether Kratom can actually kill you. After all, it's a plant, right? How dangerous can it really be? Well, according to a report from the Centers for Disease Control and Prevention (CDC) in 2019, Kratom was found to be involved in over 90 deaths in the U.S. between 2016 and 2017.

Now, before you panic and toss your Kratom stash in the bin, let's get some context. Most of these deaths involved people who were also using other substances, like opioids, alcohol, or benzodiazepines. However, a few cases showed that Kratom alone was likely the primary cause of death. The issue seems to lie in Kratom's ability to depress the central nervous system (remember, those opioid-like effects), which can lead to respiratory failure if you take too much.

The CDC's report basically boiled down to this: Kratom can*be deadly, especially when combined with other substances. So if you've got a habit of mixing Kratom with your Saturday night cocktails, you might want to rethink that strategy before your body decides to shut down entirely.

Kratom isn't harmless, and it can be deadly—especially if you're mixing it with other drugs or alcohol. Treat it with the caution you'd give to anything that might accidentally kill you.

Link: https://www.cdc.gov/mmwr/volumes/68/wr/mm6814a2.htm

## 5. Kratom and the Brain: The "It's All in Your Head" Problem

Finally, let's talk about your brain, because that's what Kratom really likes to mess with.

A 2019 study published in Neuropharmacology explored how Kratom affects the brain's reward pathways, and guess what? It behaves just like other addictive substances. Specifically, Kratom's alkaloids activate the same dopamine pathways that are involved in addiction to opioids and other drugs. You know dopamine—it's that fun little brain chemical that makes you feel good when you eat chocolate, get a hug, or binge-watch an entire season of The Office. Kratom hijacks that system, making your brain go, "Hey, let's do that again!"

The problem? When you flood your brain with dopamine too often, it starts to expect that rush, and then you're stuck chasing the high. Over time, the brain becomes less responsive to normal, everyday pleasures—like walking your dog, listening to music, or not being a dependent mess.

Kratom messes with your brain's reward system, and not in a good way. If you were hoping to use Kratom to "enhance your mood," just remember that eventually, your brain might stop caring about anything but Kratom.

You can search for other Kratom related studies and statistics by using any of the following sites:

- Google Scholar
- PubMed
- ScienceDirect
- JSTOR

# Chapter Nine
# Recent Calls to Ban Kratom

It's 2024, and Kratom's found itself in the crosshairs again. You'd think by now this leaf would have learned to keep a low profile, maybe take up a hobby that doesn't involve getting scrutinized by government agencies and health organizations. But no—Kratom just keeps stirring the pot, and now the calls to ban it have reached a fever pitch.

You see, the thing about Kratom is that it's been riding the line between "natural supplement" and "public health menace" for years now, and in 2024, that balancing act is starting to crumble. So what's the deal? Why is everyone so mad at Kratom again? And why does it feel like this plant is one bad news cycle away from getting kicked off the shelves entirely?

Let's break it down.

## 1. 2024: The Year of the Kratom Crackdown

First off, 2024 is looking like a pivotal year for Kratom, mainly because the U.S. Food and Drug Administration (FDA) and several other health agencies have ramped up their efforts to clamp down on its use. For years, the FDA has been playing a game of tug-of-war with Kratom advocates, warning about the risks while Kratom users swear it's a life-saving alternative to opioids. But now, the FDA seems to be leaning harder into its "Kratom is dangerous" stance, citing more cases of addiction, adverse health effects, and, in some instances, death.

In 2024, the FDA renewed its call to officially classify Kratom as a *Schedule I substance*. For those who don't speak "legalese," that's the same category as heroin, LSD, and other substances the government considers to have *no accepted medical use* and a high potential for abuse. In other words, if this classification goes through, Kratom could be banned nationwide, making it illegal to sell, possess, or distribute. If you thought buying Kratom was a bit shady before, imagine trying to get your hands on it when it's sitting on the DEA's naughty list.

Why the sudden push? Well, part of it has to do with rising concerns over public safety. As of early 2024, more reports have come out about Kratom-related deaths and hospitalizations, particularly among people who were using Kratom alongside other substances like opioids, alcohol, or even prescription meds. And even though Kratom alone isn't necessarily a death sentence, it's the combination of factors that has health officials sounding the alarm.

## 2. Kratom in the States: The Patchwork of Laws

To fully understand why 2024 feels like a make-or-break year for Kratom, you need to look at how the U.S. has been handling Kratom on a state level. It's a legal patchwork quilt that could only exist in the wonderfully chaotic world of American lawmaking. In some states, Kratom's totally legal—no issues, no questions asked. But in others, it's banned outright or heavily restricted, and 2024 is seeing more states lining up to put Kratom in the crosshairs.

In states like Alabama, Arkansas, Indiana, Vermont, and Wisconsin, Kratom is already banned, meaning you can't buy, sell, or possess it without risking a nice chat with law enforcement. In 2024, a few more states are debating whether to join that list. Colorado, for instance, has started introducing legislation to restrict sales, citing health concerns and the fact that the FDA hasn't approved Kratom for any medical use. Meanwhile, even states like Florida, which has historically been pro-Kratom, are starting to face public pressure to rethink their stance.

And let's not forget the local level—several cities and counties across the U.S. have already gone rogue and banned Kratom within their borders, regardless of what state law says. The logic? Local governments are claiming that Kratom's unregulated nature makes it a public health risk, especially when it comes to the potential for contamination with other dangerous substances like heavy metals or, in some cases, opioids. The result? A growing wave of public officials calling for stricter controls or outright bans on Kratom.

### 3. **The FDA's Long-Standing Beef with Kratom**

The FDA hasn't exactly kept its dislike for Kratom a secret. In fact, this feud goes all the way back to *2016*, when the agency first started sounding the alarm bells. Back then, the FDA issued a public health advisory about Kratom, warning that it had been linked to serious health risks, including respiratory depression, seizures, and, in extreme cases, death.

Then came *2017*, when the FDA attempted to push Kratom onto the Schedule I list for the first time. But this move was met with a massive backlash from Kratom advocates, who argued that the plant was saving lives by helping people wean off opioids. The outcry was so loud that the FDA backed off, and Kratom lived to fight another day.

Fast-forward to *2018*, and the FDA doubled down on its anti-Kratom stance, claiming that Kratom had "opioid-like properties" and should be treated with the same caution. They also published data suggesting that Kratom was responsible for nearly 50 deaths (though, again, most of these involved people who were mixing Kratom with other drugs).

Despite all of this, Kratom has remained legal on the federal level—until now. In 2024, the FDA's position hasn't softened, and this time, it seems they're pushing harder than ever to get Kratom classified as a Schedule I substance.

## 4. **The World Weighs In: Kratom Bans Outside the U.S.**

While the U.S. debate over Kratom is reaching a new boiling point, it's not the only country dealing with this leafy dilemma. In fact, several countries around the world have already made up their minds about Kratom, and most of them aren't fans.

Let's start with *Thailand*, the birthplace of Kratom. You'd think Thailand would be all about this plant, considering it's been used traditionally there for centuries. But nope! For decades, Thailand had a strict ban on Kratom due to concerns over abuse, particularly among manual laborers and rural communities. The ban was only lifted in *2021*, with Kratom now legalized for medical use but still tightly controlled. Even in its homeland, Kratom's walking a thin line.

Then there's *Australia*, where Kratom is classified as a *Schedule 9* substance, which is Aussie-speak for, "You're not getting your hands on this unless you're friends with a chemist and the law doesn't like you." The reason? Australian authorities are worried about its potential for addiction and the lack of research proving it's safe for long-term use.

Other countries, like *Malaysia* and *Myanmar*, also have bans on Kratom, mostly for public health reasons. And in *Europe*, countries like *Denmark* and *Sweden* have banned or restricted Kratom use, citing similar concerns about addiction, adverse health effects, and the lack of proper regulation.

In short, if you're planning to go on an international Kratom tour, don't. You'll run into more bans than you'll know what to do with.

## 5. **Kratom Advocates Fight Back: The Case for Keeping It Legal**

Despite the growing calls to ban Kratom, there's a vocal and passionate community of advocates who are fighting tooth and nail to keep Kratom legal. These are people who believe Kratom has legitimate medical uses, especially as an alternative to prescription opioids for managing chronic pain, anxiety, and opioid withdrawal.

Organizations like the *American Kratom Association (AKA)* have been leading the charge, arguing that Kratom has been unfairly demonized and that banning it would only drive people to more dangerous, illicit substances. They've gathered thousands of testimonials from people who claim Kratom has helped them reclaim their lives from opioid addiction and chronic pain, framing Kratom as a plant that, when used responsibly, can save lives.

The AKA is also pushing for something called the *Kratom Consumer Protection Act (KCPA)*, which would regulate Kratom products to ensure they're safe and free from contaminants. Their argument is that rather than banning Kratom outright, the government should focus on creating a legal framework that allows for its safe use, similar to how cannabis has been regulated in many states.

But as 2024 progresses, Kratom advocates are facing an uphill battle. With the FDA, state governments, and even some local governments pushing for more restrictions, it's becoming increasingly difficult to keep Kratom off the chopping block.

## 6. **What's Next for Kratom?**

So, where does all this leave Kratom in 2024? Right now, it's anyone's guess. The FDA seems determined to see Kratom classified as a Schedule I substance, and with more states and cities moving to ban or restrict it, the plant's future in the U.S. looks shakier than ever.

For now, Kratom users are caught in limbo, wondering if their favorite supplement is about to become a controlled substance. And while the battle rages on between advocates and government agencies, one thing is clear: Kratom's days of flying under the radar are over.

From my perspective, the Kratom ban would be an absolute win.

Here are some interesting articles you can read on the calls for bans:

1. https://today.uconn.edu/2024/02/the-kratom-controversy-nearly-2-million-americans-are-using-a-substance-banned-in-multiple-states
2. https://www.kqed.org/science/1993515/kratom-under-scrutiny-new-california-bill-proposes-stricter-controls-amid-growing-concerns
3. https://euroweeklynews.com/2024/08/29/7-recent-updates-on-kratoms-legalisation-that-you-must-know
4. https://www.authentickratom.com/education/is-kratom-legal-in-UK

# Conclusion

So, here we are—at the end of the road, the final chapter in your Kratom journey. Maybe you've read this entire book while sitting in a coffee shop, wondering if the barista could tell you're quietly freaking out about your next Kratom fix. Or maybe you're sitting at home with a cup of Kratom tea in one hand, debating whether you should finish the bag or toss it into the trash. Either way, congratulations on getting this far! You've made it through the facts, the warnings, the science, and (hopefully) a few well-placed jokes.

Now comes the hard part: figuring out what to do next.

**What Have We Learned?**

Let's take a quick recap. Kratom is not a harmless herbal supplement you can sprinkle into your life without consequences. Sure, it starts off as this intriguing "natural remedy" that promises pain relief, relaxation, and an escape from the soul-sucking routine of modern existence. To me, Kratom morphed into a devil plant — one that toyed menacingly with my life and happiness. The deeper you dive into Kratom, the more you realize it's not just a plant—it's a chemical cocktail that, for some people, can become an addictive crutch.

Throughout the chapters, we've explored the science behind Kratom's effects on your body and brain. We've talked about addiction, the physical toll it can take (hello, liver toxicity), and even the darker side of its legal status, with bans popping up faster than new coffee shop trends. We've covered dosing, withdrawal, and—let's be real—

some truly horrifying side effects that could make you second-guess your choice to dabble in the green powder.

I'm not here to shame anyone for trying Kratom. Maybe it helped you deal with chronic pain when nothing else worked, or maybe it gave you a temporary boost when you needed it most. But the reality is, for a lot of people, Kratom can slowly morph from a helpful tool into a dependency. If you've found yourself on that slippery slope, you're not alone. Plenty of people have been exactly where you are—realizing that quitting isn't as easy as they thought and wondering what to do next.

## Quitting Kratom: The First Step is Admitting You Want to Stop

The decision to quit Kratom is a big one. It's not just about stopping a habit—it's about taking control of your life again, about choosing not to let a plant (and let's face it, a pretty ugly one at that) dictate your mental and physical well-being. But here's the thing: quitting is hard. You already know that. You've read about the withdrawal symptoms, the cravings, and the mental fog that can descend when you try to kick the habit. But just because it's hard doesn't mean it's impossible.

For some, the realization that Kratom has taken over their life is enough to stop cold turkey. Others might need a more gradual approach, like tapering off or seeking medical help. Wherever you fall on that spectrum, know this: quitting Kratom isn't about being "strong enough" or having "more willpower." It's about finding the right strategy for *you*.

And maybe, just maybe, it's about knowing when to ask for help. Because let's face it—most people don't quit something like Kratom on their own. They need a support system, whether that's a friend, a counselor, or a group of people who've been through it before.

### 3. **Finding Support: You Don't Have to Do This Alone**

This brings me to something that's *absolutely* essential when quitting Kratom: support. No matter how you choose to quit—whether it's cold turkey, tapering, or with medical supervision—having people who understand what you're going through can make all the difference. Thankfully, we live in the age of the internet, where finding support has never been easier. Here are a few places you can turn to when you're ready to ditch Kratom for good:

- ***Online Communities: Reddit & Social Media Groups***

Believe it or not, there are entire online communities dedicated to helping people quit Kratom. On *Reddit*, you'll find subreddits like **r/quittingkratom** and **r/KratomRecovery**, where users share their experiences, offer advice, and most importantly, provide encouragement. You'll find everything from tips on dealing with withdrawal symptoms to personal stories that will remind you you're not the only one going through this. The beauty of these communities is their honesty—people don't sugarcoat their experiences, so you'll get a real sense of what it takes to quit and how others have managed to do it.

Other platforms like *Facebook* also have groups dedicated to quitting Kratom, where you can post anonymously if you're not ready to go public with your decision. It's all about finding a community that fits your needs, whether that's a place to vent, ask questions, or just read what others have gone through.

- **Subreddits**: r/quittingkratom and r/KratomRecovery
- **Facebook**: Search for groups like **Kratom Withdrawal and Recovery** or **Quitting Kratom Support**

- ### *The American Kratom Association (AKA)*

The *American Kratom Association* is a major player in the world of Kratom advocacy, but it also provides resources for people who are struggling with their use. While the AKA focuses on ensuring safe and regulated access to Kratom, it also recognizes that not everyone has a positive experience. They offer educational resources about safe use and tapering strategies, and they can point you in the direction of medical professionals who are Kratom-literate—meaning they understand how the plant works and how to help you quit without treating you like you've just rolled out of a heroin den.

**Website**: American Kratom Association

- ### *Therapy and Counseling: Professional Help*

If you're finding that quitting Kratom is taking a serious toll on your mental or physical health, it might be time to talk to a professional. And no, I don't mean just talking to someone who'll give you vague advice like, "Just stay positive!" I mean finding a counselor or therapist who specializes in addiction, someone who can help you work through the psychological challenges of quitting. You're not just quitting a habit—you're rewiring how your brain thinks about relief, pleasure, and stress.

There's no shame in seeking professional help. In fact, it's one of the most effective ways to ensure you quit for good. Whether it's cognitive behavioral therapy (CBT), support groups like *SMART Recovery*, or just working with a therapist who knows their way around dependency issues, getting the right help can be a game-changer.

- **Find a therapist**: Use the Psychology Today Therapist Directory
- **SMART Recovery**: www.smartrecovery.org

## The Importance of a Plan: Don't Wing It

Let's get something straight: quitting Kratom without a plan is a recipe for failure. You don't just wake up one day, throw out your stash, and expect to coast through withdrawal on a cloud of positive vibes. You need to have a strategy in place, or else you'll find yourself back in the same cycle before you can say "just one more dose."

Here's what a solid plan looks like:

1. **Set a Quit Date**: Pick a date and stick to it. Don't push it back every time you feel the temptation to delay the process.

2. **Prepare for Withdrawal**: Stock up on things that can help ease the physical symptoms—ginger tea for nausea, electrolyte drinks for hydration, over-the-counter painkillers for aches, and, most importantly, a Netflix queue full of distraction

material.

3. **Tell Someone**: Letting someone close to you know that you're quitting Kratom adds a layer of accountability. Whether it's a friend, partner, or family member, having someone check in on you can make all the difference.

4. **Focus on Small Wins**: Don't think about quitting as a giant, insurmountable mountain. Focus on getting through the next few hours, then the next day, and eventually, the next week. Celebrate the small victories—each one is a step closer to regaining control of your life.

## The Light at the End of the Tunnel

Here's the good news: it gets better. I know that right now, the idea of quitting Kratom might feel like staring down a long, painful road, but the thing about withdrawal and recovery is that they're temporary. Your body and brain will adjust. The cravings will fade. And slowly, you'll start to feel like yourself again—just without the constant need for a plant-based fix.

The point is, quitting Kratom isn't the end of your story. It's just a chapter. And trust me, the next chapter—the one where you're free from dependency, where you've got your life back—is going to be a hell of a lot better than this one.

Quitting Kratom is hard, but it's not impossible. Whether you've been using it for months or years, the fact that you're reading this right now means you've already taken the first step—you're thinking about quitting. And that's huge.

Now, it's time to take the next step. Use the resources, find your support, and most importantly, remember that you're not alone. There are thousands of people out there who've been exactly where you are, and they've come out the other side stronger for it.

So go on—take that leap.

Made in United States
Troutdale, OR
10/04/2024

23387515R00040